Dear Zoë

I so enjoyed doing your HEBREW ABC!

This one is from AFRICA

Love Debs + Chris + AIDAN

xxx

an
AFRICAN
ABC

featuring
CHRISTOPHER, LAUREN & THE CAT
Written and illustrated by Jacqui Taylor

for Nana, GG and Frances,
for all that you were to all of us

A is for adventure, the African kind,
Ancient rock art, archeological find.
Aardvark and antlion, ants all a-crawl,
Acacia above them, thorny and tall.

a
a

B is for buffalo, benignly bovine,
Baskets and beads in dazzling designs.
B is for baobab, beneath which they braaied,
Brother baboon is hidden inside.

C is for cosmos, crystal clear air,
C is for crochet, crafted with care.
Chameleon creeping, chickens a-cheep,
A drink from a calabash; cool, clean and sweet.

D is for a dusty drive on a donkey-cart at dawn,
Duiker in the long grass, dew on devil thorn.
Doves dreamily cooing, the travellers drove across the plain,
The dassies watched them coming from their lofty, dry domain.

E is for the egrets in the elephant-apple tree,
Eagerly awaiting the first discovery,
Of an excavated emerald, elegant and green,
While an evasive elephant tries not to be seen.

F is for flamboyant and flame lily red,
Free from frustration, gone fishing instead.
Find a friendly flamingo, fraternize with a frog,
But do not be fooled by what looks like a log.

G is for game park that we travelled through,
Graceful giraffe and gambolling gnu.
Through golden grass, guinea fowl and gazelle,
A great gift nature gives us, we must guard it well.

H is for hornets, a hide in a tree,
A huge hippopotamus wallows with glee.
H is for hakata see how they fall,
Hear hornbills hooting, the hoopoe's sad call.

I is for an interesting evening indaba,
Silhouette in the last light, a grazing impala.
Incandescent the flame, insects in flight,
Ibis alight in wait for the night.

J is for jubilation, join in the jamboree,
Jungle drums are drumming under the jacaranda tree.
Jump like a jerboa, as joyful as a jay,
Java prints all jitterbug and jive the day away.

K is for Kariba Dam, kapenta caught at night,
Kiewietjie and kestrel, kingfisher and kite.
A kraal upon the kopje, a kudu standing still,
Klipspringer by the lakeside bends down to drink his fill.

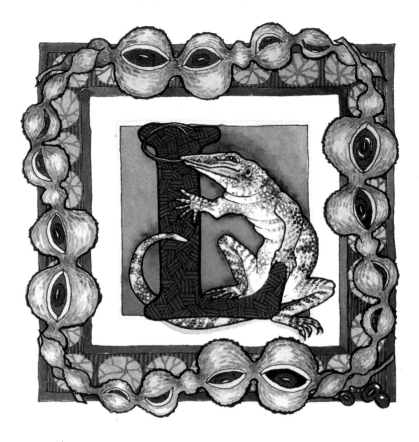

L is for Limpopo as it languidly rolls by,
Reflecting there a sky as blue as lapis lazuli.
Lizards, lions and leguvuans lie lazing in the sun,
Little children laughing, finding lucky beans for fun.
Lilac are the lilies where the lilytrotter trips,
Louries look on leisurely as past the river slips.

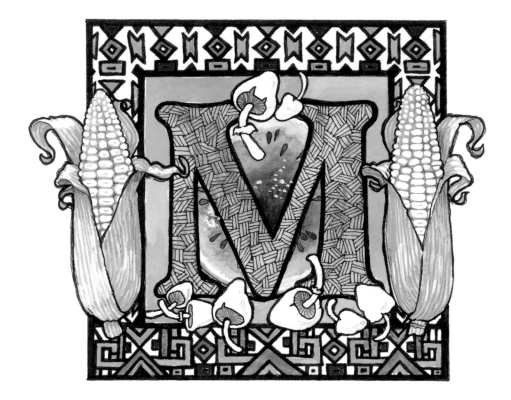

M is for market, a place we all meet,
Mielies for munching, mangoes so sweet.
Monkeys make mischief, marimbas make sound,
We move to the music that echoes all round.

N is for the nightjar, as night descends he calls,
Nagapies nestled in a tree, nearby the water falls.
N'ganga narrates an ancient tale, and gives a magic show,
Night shadows from the firelight dance and leap and grow.

O is for an ostrich who obliged them with a ride,
Outsized oval eggs hold offspring safe inside.
Onlookers observing, perched upon a pole,
An oxpecker, an owl and a golden oriole.

P is for praying mantis, with front legs raised in prayer,
Pangolin and porcupine - a most peculiar pair.
Piles of painted pottery, perfect as a present,
Poinsettia profusely blooms, pretty, pink and pleasant.

Q is for the quarry where stands the quiver tree,
Quantities of quelea quibbling with glee.
Quickly through the quaking grass slips a quavering quail.
On a quest, a quiet quintet are on the quail's trail.

R is for the river after reviving rain,
To ride a rare rhinoceros across the rambling plain.
To raft upon the rapids, with rushing, rolling speed,
To see the reedbuck running, red bishops on the reeds.

S is for Shona sculpture in springstone and serpentine,
Sabi star is shining, sunbird in sweet sunshine.
Seven secretary birds strutting solemnly,
Shamwaris sharing sadza under the spreading sausage tree.

T is for two trumpet fish floating top to toe,
A trillion tartan hawk fish darting to and fro.
Treasure for the taking, a terrific turtle ride,
Tube worms in tranquil turquoise
swishing with the tide.

U is for umbrella thorn, a most unusual tree,
The Umfolozi murmurs on its way down to the sea.
The universe unfolds above, an unbelievable array
Of stars unique and unsurpassed, the unending milky way.

V is for Victoria Falls, a view that must be seen,
The vast and vaporous waterfall, the cavernous ravine.
The rain forest so verdant, vanishing in mist,
A valiant rainbow hung above, this place that God has kissed.

W is for wire toys with wheels that wobble round,
Warthogs beneath the willow tree,
with noses to the ground.
While weavers weave their perfect nests
to lay their eggs within,
All wondering which wire toy will finish first to win.

X is for xaguxagu tree, isi xaxabesha thereupon,
Beneath, a travelling Xhosa man who sang the saddest song.
A tale of Gxara River and its lovely spirit pool,
Xyris blooming round about, the water clean and cool.

Y is for a yellowfish, yucca plant and yams,
Yellowbilled the stork and duck,
yellow yacht on yonder dam.
Yellowbellied hyliota, yellowbellied bulbul,
Yellowbellied flycatcher catching flies till he is full-full.
Lesser and greater yellowlegs wade a yard from shore,
There a yellowbreasted sunbird, a yellowspotted nicator.

y

y

y

y

Z is for the zebra that the Zulu rode with zest,
To Zambia and Zimbabwe and those lands he loves best.
The sun was at its zenith, the day was warm and bright,
As the Zulu read his favourite book with a zealous delight.

Glossary

Aa

aardvark
antbear or anteater. Seldom seen, the aardvark is a solitary, nocturnal and shy animal. It is usually about 1.5 m long and weighs about 50 kgs. The aardvark lives almost exclusively on ants and termites, which it catches on its long, sticky tongue. Aardvarks live in a series of excavated burrows in woodland or grassland areas.

acacia
a large tree, the most common species being the *Acacia Karroo* or mimosa thorn. There are long white spines on the branches, the pods are sickle-shaped, the leaves compound and the flowers spherical, yellow and fluffy.

African adventure
when we say 'Africa', we often think of its association with adventure: expeditions through jungles, safaris across wide open plains, white water rafting, hiking through rugged mountains and much more.

ancient art
rock art is to be found on many exposed granite rock faces and the walls of caves throughout southern Africa. Pigment used was taken from lichen and soil, and mixed with blood, tree sap or animal fat. Scenes usually depicted animals, humans with their tools, weapons and adornments, in hunting or ritual scenes.

antlion
the antlion larvae live half-buried in conical pits in the sand, 10 to 30 mm wide. If an ant or small insect stumbles into the pit, sand is flicked at it until it falls to the bottom. The antlion then catches it and sucks it dry. The nocturnal adult has wings that resemble a dragonfly's, but it does not fly very well.

archeological find
many artefacts of past societies have been found and recorded on archeological digs in Africa, such as cooking pots, drinking vessels, beads, tools of rock and bone and copper ingot crosses. Also recorded are rock paintings, remains of stone walling and construction or excavation of many kinds.

Bb

baboon
this species of monkey is usually found in troops of about 100 within a home range of several square kilometres. Baboons will eat almost any type of plant or vegetable matter. This makes them a pest for farmers, in addition to the fact that they will take poultry. They also eat reptiles, insects and the young of small antelope. The male can reach a length of 1.5 m and a weight of 30 kgs.

baobab	adult baobabs have stout trunks which are able to store water. Trees with diameters of over 10 m may be more than 2 000 years old. The hollow inside of one old tree has been used as a bus shelter. The young trees look so different from the adults, that this may have led to the traditional belief that an angry god planted the adult trees upside down. The baobab has large, white flowers and a bulbous fruit with a hard shell containing many seeds coated with cream of tartar.
baskets and beads	a vast range of baskets is to be found, each suited to a particular domestic use. Shape, size and design depend on which ethnic group has made the basket and which materials and dyes have been used. Beadwork also varies greatly in function and design throughout southern Africa. Beads are not only used to make necklaces, collars and bracelets, but are stitched onto ceremonial clothing or joined to make beaded aprons.
benignly bovine	although buffalo may appear as tame and docile as domestic cattle, they are not tame and can kill if approached or startled by a human.
braaied	'braaivleis' is a word of Afrikaans origin, quite literally meaning 'cook meat', and it is the equivalent of a European barbecue. 'Boerewors' is standard fare at a 'braaivleis' and it means 'farmer sausage'.
buffalo	this is a member of the subfamily *Bovinae*, which includes cattle and the Asiatic buffalo. Buffalo are usually found grazing in grassland near water. Males can weigh up to 800 kg and have much darker colouring and heavier horns than their female companions. Bachelors or wounded animals can be very aggressive.

Cc

calabash	a hole is cut in a gourd with a hard outer skin. The soft inside is scooped out and the hollow gourd is used to carry water or as a drinking vessel.
chameleon	a member of the lizard family, this strange creature has independently rotating eyes and the ability to change its colour to that of its environment. It lives on insects, largely grasshoppers, which it catches with a sticky tongue as long as its body. The chameleon has a prehensile tail that helps it to climb. Local people have a superstition that a chameleon is an ancestor reincarnated.
chickens	most rural people in Africa keep a few chickens for eggs and meat. In outlying areas chickens can be seen scratching for grubs at the roadside.
cosmos	from February to April these lovely flowers grow by the roadside and on open ground. They range from deep pink through to white.
crochet	an astonishing array of garments, tablecloths, bedspreads and placemats are crochet-crafted by the local women and sold at roadside markets.

Dd

dassies
these mammals are known by several names – rock rabbit, rock hyrax, stone badger and the biblical name, coney. They have the appearance of rodents, but are tailless and quite large – 30 to 50 cm long. They live on rocky outcrops in colonies ranging from a few to several hundred individuals. They eat grass, seeds, leaves and fruit.

devil thorn
an indigenous, ground-hugging creeper, with trumpet-shaped, mauve flowers and deadly, double thorns on its seeds.

donkey cart
much more in use earlier in the 20th century, for the carriage of produce and people, these donkey-drawn, wooden carts can still be seen in rural areas and smaller towns.

duiker
this small, solitary antelope is widespread and can often be seen on farmland or on the perimeters of suburban areas. The common duiker stands about 50 cm at the shoulder and weighs about 15 kg. It eats flowers, fruits, seeds, leaves and twigs, and can cause much damage to crops.

Ee

egrets
the egrets featured in the illustration are cattle egrets, common companions to livestock grazing in open grassland. The birds eat insects disturbed by the movement of the livestock and pluck ticks from the hides of the animal, hence the name 'tick bird'. They form huge egretries in trees, usually above or near water, where they nest and roost.

elephant
the largest of the land mammals, weighing up to 7 000 kg and living up to 70 years of age. Elephants eat plant material, and because of their size, must eat for up to 18 hours a day to maintain their strength. To find water they may travel up to 80 km a day, drinking as much as 200 litres at one time. A single calf is born after a gestation period of 22 months. Elephants have been hunted for many years by poachers for the ivory of their tusks. However, an international ban on ivory trade has slowed down this activity in recent years.

elephant-apple tree
its botanical name is *Strychnos spinosa*, also called the monkey orange or matamba by young Ndebele children, who use the round fruit as playthings. The unripe, green fruit is bitter, but when the fruit turns yellow, the hard shell is cracked open and the sweet sticky inside is eaten. This fruit also has several traditional medicinal uses.

emerald
a brilliant green gemstone mined in Africa. Emeralds are usually cut and sold to dealers in London or Zürich and set into contemporary jewellery.

excavate
to reveal or extract by digging.

Ff

fishing
a favourite pastime in southern Africa's many dams and rivers. Freshwater fish include bream, barbel, bass, trout, nkupi, chessa and stickleback, to name a few.

flamboyant
this spectacular flowering tree originates from Madagascar. It is now found extensively throughout southern Africa, lining streets and gracing gardens with a festival of red flowers. It can grow up to 15 m in height and has long, brown seed pods that take up to two years to mature.

flame lily
or *Gloriosa superba*, is the national flower of Zimbabwe and can be found blooming wild during the rainy season, but picking it is forbidden as it is a protected species.

flamingo
two species of flamingo occur in southern Africa. They are transient visitors mainly during the dry season and may be found in large flocks that frequent brackish water. They feed with their bills upside down, sieving small animals and plants from the water with the aid of a large tongue.

frog
many species of frog and toad occur in southern Africa. They are aquatic breeders whose diet consists largely of insects caught on the end of a long, sticky tongue. Large species will also eat other frogs, rodents, chicks and small snakes. They themselves are preyed upon by birds, snakes and large lizards.

Gg

gazelle
a small graceful antelope – several species are found in southern Africa.

giraffe
these are the tallest animals in the world: a full-grown male stands at over 5 m and weighs over 1 000 kg. Giraffes browse in dry savannah and are partial to the leaves of the acacia tree.

gnu
the migratory blue wildebeest or brindled gnu are found in herds of 40 or more. They graze in savannah woodland close to plentiful surface water. Adult males stand about 1.5 m at the shoulder and weigh up to 250 kg.

guinea fowl
two species are found in southern Africa, the helmeted guinea fowl and the crested guinea fowl. The more common helmeted species is found on farmland and in wildlife areas throughout southern Africa. It can be found in fairly large flocks, except during the breeding season, and spends most of its time on the ground, rarely flying. The guinea fowl feeds on insects, seeds and tubers, or gleans food from the croplands.

Gxara River	meaning 'river of the precipice', is in the old Transkei area of South Africa. In the river is a pool surrounded by trees and flowering plants, where a medium named Nonquawuse came to bathe. While gazing into the water, she claimed to see the faces of ancestral spirits and to hear voices – telling her that they would help to drive away white settlers. But, as a sign of faith, the Xhosa people were to destroy all their cattle and crops. A fever of killing and destruction began. But on the promised day, 18 February 1857, the cattle, new crops and armies of reincarnated warriors failed to appear. Luckily one section of the tribe remained aloof to the predictions, and through their compassion many were saved that would have died. It is estimated that 25 000 people died of starvation. Many were also saved by the settlers who helped to feed them. The discredited medium fled, but was arrested by police, and spent the rest of her days on a farm near King William's Town.

Hh

hakata	the name given to the divining instruments used by Shona n'gangas or spirit mediums. A set consists of four flat dice, intricately carved to represent the male and female domain. These are 'treated', thrown and their meaning is interpreted according to how they are lying.
hide	a structure built to blend in with the natural surroundings, and in which people can conceal themselves to observe wildlife and birds.
hippopotamus	an amphibious mammal found in rivers and dams throughout central and southern Africa. They are found, in herds of ten to 15, in areas where there are permanent stretches of water. A lot of time is spent under the water where paths on the river or lakebed are made, just as on land. Hippopotami can eat up to 130 kg of vegetation in a night, are quite territorial and can be dangerous, especially to boats, canoes, and their occupants.
hoopoe	the hoopoe's name derives from its call. It is found throughout southern Africa in open woodland, tree savannah and suburban gardens. A hoopoe feeds largely on insect larvae dug from the ground with its long bill. Its fan-shaped crest is raised when the bird is alarmed.
hornbill	this bird has an outsized bill and a raucous call. There are nine species of hornbill found in southern Africa, found mainly in forest or dense woodland. They feed on small reptiles, fruit and insects.

Ii

ibis	the ibis and the spoonbill are of the same family and five species are found in southern Africa. The ibis is characterized by a long, down-

curved bill. They are gregarious birds and may be found roosting in huge flocks, usually along rivers, near ponds or dams. Their diet consists mainly of frogs, beetles and worms.

impala

seen in herds of between five and 30, and up to several hundred in the dry season, impala are found mainly in woodland areas in the wild. They are also popular animals for game ranching, and are cropped for meat and skins.

incandescent

the shining or glowing produced by the filament of a lamp.

indaba

this is a commonly used Nguni word for a meeting or discussion. Under 'Indaba Tree', now a national monument, the Ndebele king, Lobengula, frequently held meetings. In 1896, Cecil Rhodes held peace negotiations with Ndebele leaders in the Matopo Hills. These negotiations are now popularly termed 'The Great Indaba'.

insects

the class *Insecta* is the largest class in the animal kingdom, comprising 75 to 80% of all animal species. Insects in Africa are diverse and prolific, particularly during the wet season. Mosquitoes, gnats, moths, butterflies, beetles, mantids, grasshoppers, flies, ants and a host of other bugs are to be found.

isi xaxabesha

the Xhosa name for the capped wheatear. This bird, common throughout southern Africa, can be found around homes, deserted camp sites and cattle kraals – anywhere where the earth is bare or the grass short. It hops about with much tail and wing flicking, flies up and back down with outbursts of song, readily imitates other bird calls and even the noises of farm animals. It feeds on flies, locusts and ants.

Jj

jacaranda

this tree originates from Brazil but is now to be found extensively throughout central and southern Africa. The showy clusters of mauve, trumpet-shaped flowers appear from late September through to December, turning the larger trees into beautiful clouds of colour.

jamboree

celebration, merry-making.

Java print

a length of Java worn as a wrap is almost national dress in Zimbabwe. Characterized by bright geometric designs and motifs, the cloth is also made up into all sorts of clothing and decorative linen.

jay

the lilac-breasted rollers illustrated are sometimes incorrectly termed blue jays because of their bright plumage and aerobatic flight displays. They live largely on insects, lizards, small rodents and birds. Of the 11 species of roller in the world, six occur in southern Africa.

jerboa	this is a small jumping rodent that lives in the desert. It is in fact not a southern African creature at all, but north African in origin.
jubilation	rejoicing, exultation.
jungle drums	drums vary greatly in size, shape and design, but are usually made by hollowing a section of soft wood, then stretching a well-treated, wet skin over the hollow and securing it with pegs. The skin is then carefully heated until it grows taut and the desired sound is acquired.

Kk

kapenta	this fish is also known as the Lake Tanganyika sardine, from where it was introduced into the Kariba Dam. It is caught on a commercial basis by both Zimbabwean and Zambian fisheries. The fish, once caught, are brined and sun-dried on racks, bagged and sold. Some are frozen, canned or used as crocodile food.
Kariba Dam	one of the largest man-made lakes in the world, with a maximum capacity of 180 600 million cubic metres. Built between 1955 and 1959 on the Zambezi River to supply hydroelectric power to Zambia and Zimbabwe, it is a popular place for watersport, fishing and game-viewing.
kestrel	the kestrel is a small predatory bird. Several species, usually migratory, are to be found in southern Africa; locations, habits and diet vary according to the type of kestrel. Food ranges from termites, insects, frogs and lizards to crabs, small mammals and occasionally birds. Usually considered valuable birds, kestrels are protected by sentiment and sometimes by law.
kiewietjie	there are several species of kiewietjie, or plover, found in southern Africa. The more common of these being the crowned plover and the blacksmith plover. Both these species will swoop down on an intruder, uttering harsh cries if they feel their young or eggs are threatened. They nest on the ground near water and eat insects (such as grasshoppers and beetles), worms and small molluscs.
kingfisher	11 species occur in southern Africa, mostly brightly coloured with long bills. Kingfishers are found near water and dive for their food – frogs, crabs and fish – from a perch. There are some woodland species, however, who subsist on insects and grubs.
kite	there are several species of kite in southern Africa. Predatory birds, they feed on rodents, lizards, bats, carrion and sometimes insects.
klipspringer	a small buck, normally found in pairs on rocky or steep terrain. Their ability to climb sometimes helps them to escape predators. Klipspringers are browsers and obtain most of their moisture requirements from their food.

kopje	a small hill or rocky outcrop.
kraal	a fenced area built of sticks and thorny branches to keep cattle and other livestock safe from predators at night. Sometimes a kraal is built to enclose a whole village, usually comprising several circular huts. Each hut is used for a specific purpose – cooking and eating, sleeping or storage.
kudu	the largest antelope found in Sub-Saharan Africa. The male stands 1.2 m at the shoulder and weighs about 250 kg. Both male and female are greyish-fawn and have vertical white stripes between the rump and the shoulder. Kudu are found in most wildlife areas and also sometimes in farming areas, where they pose a threat to crops as they can clear a 2 m fence.

Ll

lapis lazuli	a bright blue gemstone.
leguvuans	among the largest lizards in the world, they are robustly built, covered with small scales and have relatively long tails that cannot be shed. They are voracious carnivores.
lily trotter	so called because of its ability to run about nimbly on floating vegetation. This bird's proper name is the African Jacana. The female will collect a 'harem' of up to four males, defending them against other females. The male incubates the eggs and rears the young.
Limpopo	the river rises in the far north of South Africa, and forms the border between South Africa and Botswana for some distance. It also forms part of Zimbabwe's southern border with South Africa. The Limpopo flows into the Indian Ocean just north of Maputo in Mozambique.
lion	the largest African carnivore, lions occur in woodland, scrub and grassland. Their prey ranges in size from insects, to animals as large as buffalo and giraffe. Most kills are made by female lionesses working together as a team. Prides can number up to 30. An adult male stands 1.25 m at the shoulder and weighs up to 230 kg.
lizards	none of the species found in Africa is venomous. They can shed their tails when attacked, allowing them to escape, and then grow a new tail. Species represented in southern Africa include geckos, chameleons, skinks, agamas, common, girdled and plated lizards and leguvuans or monitors. Generally, lizards are carnivorous and reproduce by means of laying eggs.
lourie	this is an exclusively African bird, 22 species of which are to be found in Africa, five in southern Africa: Ross' lourie, the purple-crested lourie, the Knysna lourie, the grey lourie and Livingstone's lourie. The grey

lourie is also called the 'go-away' bird because of its loud, distinctive call. They are clumsy fliers and are much more nimble running along or hopping amongst the branches. They eat fruit, birds and insects and are usually found in groups of two or more.

lucky beans
lucky beans come from the tree *Erythrina abyssinica*, widespread throughout southern Africa. The hard red beans are used decoratively to make necklaces, as eyes for toys, and are sometimes set in clear resin as keyrings, bangles or ashtrays. The wood of the tree is used for making toys, stools and drums. It was also used as brake blocks for wagons.

Mm

mangoes
the mango tree is an evergreen tree that originates in India and south east Asia, but is now grown throughout the tropics. There are several different varieties. The delicious, yellow flesh can be eaten raw when the fruit is ripe; cooked or made into chutney.

marimba
the marimba, or African xylophone, consists of a solid framework attached to which is a set of between ten and 22 hardwood keys, and a set of different-sized gourds, usually pumpkin shells, for resonance. The keys are struck with two lengths of wood with rounded wooden heads.

mealies
maize or corn forms the staple diet of the majority of the people of central and southern Africa. Cultivation is undertaken by both large-scale commercial farmers and the individual growing for his own needs. It can be eaten boiled or roasted on the cob. However, much of it is ground to make mealie meal for sadza (see sadza). It is also used as stock feed.

Milky Way
the Milky Way is our galaxy. It is a typical spiral galaxy of about 100 000 light years in diameter and 15 000 light years thick at its centre. To us it appears as a band across the sky as we view it from its centre.

Nn

n'ganga
a witch doctor, diviner or medium who has a talent for healing, divined through a spirit. Strictly speaking, n'gangas should only diagnose illness and give advice on who to consult for treatment. In practice, however, most n'gangas both divine (by throwing bones or hakata) and prescribe (usually some form of 'muti' or medicine made from indigenous plants and other materials).

nagapie
night ape or bushbaby. They are sometimes kept as pets – although this should be discouraged because of the animals' habit of washing in their own urine and jumping wildly, causing disruption. Nagapies are found in family groups of two to six in woodland areas and feed on insects and exuded gum from trees.

night jar	a nocturnal bird, seven species of which are found in southern Africa. Dull-looking, brown and grey birds with flecks of black and white, they are better known for their persistent, mournful call than for appearance. They catch insects in flight just before dawn and at dusk. They are often hit by cars at night, as they sit on the road absorbing the residual warmth of the sun.
Nyangombe Falls	one of the many picturesque waterfalls at Nyanga, Zimbabwe, rushing down over steeply terraced granite rocks.

Oo

offspring	the ostrich lays a clutch of four to eight eggs, guarded and incubated by the parents in turn. When the young are born they are fuzzy and greyish brown in colour.
oriole	four species of this bird occur in southern Africa. Their name is derived from the Latin word meaning 'golden'. Orioles are usually found in woodland areas near water, and they feed on fruit and insects.
ostrich	the ostrich is the largest living bird in the world. It is flightless and fairly common in grassland or lightly wooded savannah, feeding on vegetation and occasionally insects. The male is about 2 m in height and weighs up to 150 kg. He is mainly black in colour with white feathers on the wings and tail, while the female is greyish-brown. Ostriches are found in groups of five to ten, except during the breeding season when they pair. During breeding the male is very aggressive – a kick from an ostrich can be lethal. Ranching of the ostrich is on the increase, for the feathers, meat and skin, which is used as leather.
outsized oval eggs	because of their size and strength, ostrich eggs have been used since the early Stone Age for carrying and storing water, and for making beads. Shells are now blown and sold as curios, sometimes decorated with painting or beadwork.
owl	12 species of owl occur in southern Africa. They are mainly nocturnal birds that prey on rodents, amphibians and insects. Distinctive by their round, forward-facing eyes set in a pronounced facial disc, owls also have sharp beaks and talons.
oxpecker	there are two species of oxpecker that occur in southern Africa. These birds are best known for the the symbiotic relationship that they have with many of the larger mammals, riding on and removing ticks and parasites from the host animal. Oxpeckers also serve as an early warning system of danger to the host, flying up and hissing, causing the host animal to seek cover.

Pp

pangolin
the pangolin is a reserved, nocturnal mammal. Its body, legs and tail are covered with heavy, brown scales. When alarmed, it rolls itself up into an armoured ball. It has strong claws for digging into anthills and licks up the ants with its very long, sticky tongue. Found in woodlands and rocky terrain, the pangolin has significant traditional importance, and can often be presented to chiefs or spirit mediums as a gift.

poinsettia
a shrub that blooms in profusion in suburbia during the winter months. The showy flowers occur in several colours – red, peach, pink and white.

porcupine
the porcupine occurs widely and is actually a large rodent. It is covered in stiff, black hair and on the tail, back and head are black and white spines used for defence. If cornered, the porcupine raises its spines and runs sideways or backwards into its aggressor, usually inflicting severe injury. Porcupines are mainly nocturnal and feed on roots and tubers.

pottery
traditional pots have been fashioned out of clay in Africa for thousands of years. Nowadays, a lot of pottery is made, painted, fired and sold commercially, both for the local and domestic markets, or for export.

praying mantis
the mantis is an insect that feeds on other insects and spiders. When in ambush, it holds its specially adapted forelegs slightly forward and together, as if in prayer – hence the name. The female mantis will sometimes eat the male during mating. Their forewings are often coloured or shaped like dead or living leaves for disguise.

Qq

quail
these birds are found in grassland and spending more time on the ground than in flight. They are game birds often shot for sport. They feed on seeds, insects and vegetable matter.

quarry
the most impressive quarries have been formed where the granite bedrock has been blasted away to supply granite blocks or chips for building. A large hole is left, often with a pool of water at the bottom.

quelea
the red-billed quelea is widespread throughout Africa. At a distance, a flock can appear to be a cloud of smoke, so large are the numbers of birds, ranging from a few thousand to hundreds of thousands. They are comparable to locusts in the destruction they can cause to crops – feeding almost exclusively on seeds and grain. Sometimes the weight of a roosting flock can break the branches of a tree. Occasionally, dynamite is set in a tree in which they roost, and is detonated at night to rid the farmer of the pest.

quintet	a group of five.
quiver tree	so called because the bushmen made pincushion-type quivers from its fibrous core. Also known as the kokerboom, this tree thrives on the west coast of South Africa and can store water, making it resistant to drought.

Rr

raft	rafting on white water in Africa is a popular, exhilarating pastime.
red bishop birds	the male is distinctive by his black forehead and bright red plumage. The red bishop bird is common throughout southern Africa and in some parts is considered to be a pest by farmers. Its favoured nesting site is in amongst reeds, but it has also taken to nesting in standing corn. The male is polygamous and will have several mates. These birds can occur in very small or very large flocks.
reedbuck	the name comes from this animal's preference to remain near water in amongst reedbeds, grass or vlei. Predominantly grazers, reedbuch are found in small groups or pairs. Males stand about 90 cm at the shoulder and weigh about 80 kg.
reviving rain	because Africa is so prone to drought, at the end of the dry season, the start of the rains is always cause for celebration.
rhinoceros	this is the second largest land mammal and an endangered species. Two species occur in Africa, the black rhino and the white rhino. A white rhino bull can weigh up to 2 300 kg, a black rhino bull up to 1 000 kg. They are both grazers found in woodland or dense bush. The white rhino is more likely to be found in groups than the black rhino, which is more solitary. The black rhino is subject to poaching, the horns finding markets in the Middle and Far East.

Ss

Sabi star	this is a succulent shrub or dwarf tree with a smooth, silvery-green trunk. It is found in the Sabi and Zambezi Valleys and produces very pretty white flowers with a frilled, crimson rim.
sadza	this is the staple diet of the majority of the central and southern African populations. Maize meal or mealie meal is mixed with water and a little salt, and is cooked to form a thick porridge, eaten with the hands and dipped into relish, sour milk or stew.
sausage tree	this large tree has beautiful maroon flowers and heavy seedpods, up to 1 m in length, that resemble sausages or cucumbers. The unripe fruit

is very poisonous, but the ripe fruit is baked and put into traditional beer to aid fermentation. It is also used in powdered form on sores, or the seeds roasted and eaten if other food is scarce. One traditional belief from southern part of Zimbabwe is that one piece of the fruit, hung inside a hut, will protect against damage by whirlwinds, which the people there fear deeply. Dr. Livingstone camped under, and carved his initials on, a sausage tree just prior to seeing the Victoria Falls for the first time.

secretary bird

this tall bird gets its name from its long, drooping crest feathers, reminiscent of 19th-century clerks who would keep their feather quills behind their ears. Secretary birds are usually found in pairs within a large territory, with a central roosting and nesting tree. They feed on small mammals, reptiles, birds and insects.

shamwari

the Shona word for friend.

Shona sculpture

most of this carving is done in soapstone, serpentine, granite or springstone. Stone sculpture originally depicted animals and creatures from Shona mythology in Zimbabwe, but has, particularly post-independence, begun to show more of the individual sculptors' personal style and vision. Shona sculpture is now internationally recognised, shown and appreciated.

sunbird

21 species of sunbird occur in southern Africa. They are small, pretty birds with long, thin, curved bills used to probe flowers for nectar. The males usually sport several different bright colours, often metallic in appearance.

Tt

tartan hawk fish

(*Oxycirrhites typus*) this reef dweller is decorated with grids of bright colour that provide it with a good disguise when it is against the spread of a sea fan of the same colour.

trumpet fish

(*Aulostomus*) the trumpet fish is a predator. To hunt, it uses the cover of a large, non-threatening fish such as the parrot fish. It curves its long slender body closely against that of the parrot fish, and when it spots suitable prey, breaks cover to grab itself a meal. It has the habit of resting with its nose down in the coral.

tube worms

tube worms burrow into coral and establish themselves as a colony. They retract their pretty feathery tentacles into their tubes for protection if touched.

turtle

there are several different types of sea turtle. Green turtle, leatherback turtle, loggerhead turtle and olive ridley turtle, to name a few. Turtles return to the same breeding grounds every year by some inbuilt navigation system. Female turtles, carrying eggs that have been fertilised at sea, return to the same beach on which they were born to lay their eggs. They come up onto the beach at night, sometimes in their hundreds, dig a hole and deposit about a 100 eggs into the hole, which they then cover. The incubation period is about 50 days and when the baby turtles hatch, they head instinctively for the sea. Many of them are eaten by predators before they even reach the sea.

Uu

umbrella thorn   Haak-en-steek is the Afrikaans name for this tree and its botanical name is *Acacia tortilis*. It is found widely in southern Africa, distinctive by its flat top. The bark, pods and leaves are eaten by wild and domestic animals alike, and the wood is often used for fuel. The tree also provides an excellent nesting site for birds.

Umfolozi   this is one of the major rivers in South Africa and means 'zigzag' river in Zulu, because of its complex course through the hills of KwaZulu-Natal. It is also the site of one of Africa's oldest game reserves where rhinos, elephants, lions, buffaloes and leopards can be found.

universe   the word means everything that exists in creation. In relation to all that is out there; planets, stars, moons, galaxies, black holes and UFOs, the earth is minute. There have been different perceptions of the universe throughout the ages, what it is and how it operates. The advent of the modern telescope, the computer and space travel have all helped us to gain much more knowledge about the universe.

Vv

valiant   brave or bold.

Victoria Falls   located on the Zambezi River, these falls are Zimbabwe's best-known feature and tourist attraction. With a width of 1 700 m and an average depth of 100 m, they form the biggest curtain of falling water in the world and are indeed one of the seven wonders of the natural world.

Ww

warthog   a wild pig, found in family groups in most wildlife areas, and some of the more remote farming areas. The warthog has become popular with the game ranching industry because they breed well and their meat is palatable. Boars are about 70 cm at the shoulder and weigh about 100 kg. A disc-shaped nose is adapted for digging up grass rhizomes. Warthogs also feed on grasses, fruits, berries and bark. If alarmed, they trot off, with their tails held erect, giving rise to the name 'running aerials'.

weavers	these birds are sparrow-sized or slightly larger. The male of the species builds a neatly enclosed, suspended nest, often above water and a common sight in many suburban gardens. If the chosen female does not feel the nest is suitable, she will pull it down and the male will start again. During the mating season the male sings long and loudly, a lovely liquid sound.
willow tree	the weeping willow is seen frequently next to dams and rivers in southern Africa. It is, however, not an indigenous tree.
wire toys	these ingenious and unusual toys have become something of an art form in Zimbabwe and South Africa. Using straightened scrap wire, bottle tops, silver paper and other materials, a wide variety of cars, bikes, buses, helicopters, etc. are fashioned. The steering shaft is a long piece of wire attached to the front axle and reaches up to about waist-height. Originally, the toys were only made by the children for their own use. Now they are often made by vendors who sell them to passers-by on the street.

Xx

xaguxagu tree	the Ndebele word for the tree hibiscus or snot apple tree. It has showy yellow flowers with a dark red spot at the base and the fruit, surrounded by a dry furry case, is sweet and glutinous. The name 'xaguxagu' stems from the sound made whilst chewing the fruit.
Xhosa	the Xhosa people originate from the old Transkei area of South Africa. The language of these farming people is punctuated with a delightful series of clicks.
Xyris	*Xyris capensis* or yellow-eyed grass is a rushlike plant with a cluster of leaves at the base of the plant, from which comes a tall stem with a cluster of yellow flowers on the top. This species grows in marshy ground.

Yy

yams	or sweet potatoes, with a red or beige outside skin and a sweet starchy inside, are delicious baked or roasted and eaten with butter, salt and pepper.
yellow	yellowbilled stork, yellowbilled duck, yellowbilled hyliota, yellowbellied bulbul, yellowbellied fly catcher, lesser yellowlegs, greater yellowlegs, yellow breasted sunbird, yellow spotted nicator – these are all birds found in central and southern Africa.
yellowfish	the large-scale yellowfish is fairly widespread in central Africa. It prefers rocky-bottomed, fairly fast-flowing rivers and feeds on aquatic larvae and insects, shrimps, molluscs, crustacea and small fish.

yucca plant	this plant originates from the southern United States, but is found extensively throughout southern Africa. It is several metres high when fully grown, has a lot of long slim leaves at its base and a long central stem that carries bracelets of very pretty, bell-shaped white flowers.

Zz

Zambia	the countries that have common borders with Zambia are: Botswana, Zimbabwe, Mozambique, Malawi, Zaire, the Democratic Republic of Congo, Angola and Namibia. The capital of the country is Lusaka and the mainstays of the economy are copper, agriculture and tourism.
zebra	the zebra belongs to the same family as the horse and the donkey. They are easily recognisable by their bold black and white hides. There are several different species in southern Africa; Burchell's zebra, Cape zebra, Grevy's zebra, Hartmann's zebra and the quagga, now extinct. An adult zebra weighs about 300 kg. They live in family groups that often form into a larger herd that moves together. Zebra are found in woodland, scrub or grassland, always close to water. The gestation period of the female is about 12 months, after which time she gives birth to a single foal usually born in the rainy season.
zealous	to have great enthusiasm and passion about an activity or sphere of interest.
zenith	that point of the heavens directly above an observer.
Zimbabwe	Zimbabwe has common borders with Zambia, Mozambique, South Africa and Botswana. The capital city is Harare and it relies on agriculture, tourism and mineral wealth to sustain its economy.
Zulu	famed for their bravery and stamina in battle, the Zulu are probably the largest single population group in South Africa. The group's origin lies in a small Nguni-speaking chiefdom that emerged in what is now KwaZulu-Natal, in the 16th century. In 1818 the famous Shaka became chief of the group, and transformed it into the Zulu nation, the mightiest empire in southern Africa.

Struik Lifestyle
(an imprint of Random House Struik (Pty) Ltd)
Company Reg. No. 1966/003153/07
80 McKenzie Street, Cape Town 8001
PO Box 1144, Cape Town, 8000, South Africa

First published by Printline Ltd, Hong Kong in 1996
Second edition published by Struik Publishers in 2001
Reprinted in 2004, 2005, 2006, 2007, 2008
Reprinted by Struik Lifestyle in 2009

ISBN 978-1-86872-703-2

Publisher: Linda de Villiers
Managing editor: Cecilia Barfield
Designer and illustrator: Jacqui Taylor
DTP: Sean Robertson
Reproduction: Printline Ltd, Hong Kong
Printing and binding: Sing Cheong Printing Company Limited